LIGHTING UP THE SKY

LIGHTNING

SETH KINGSTON

PowerKiDS press.
New York

Published in 2021 by The Rosen Publishing Group, Inc.
29 East 21st Street, New York, NY 10010

First Edition

Portions of this work were originally authored by Kristen Rajczak and published as *Lightning*. All new material in this edition authored by Seth Kingston.

Editor: Elizabeth Krajnik
Book Design: Reann Nye

Photo Credits: Cover jerbarber/iStock/Getty Images Plus/Getty Images; series art Zoteva/Shutterstock.com; series art Abstractor/Shutterstock.com; p. 5 (top) Nolan Caldwell/Moment/Getty Images; p. 5 (bottom) photominer/Shutterstock.com; p. 7 Francesco Iemma/EyeEm/Getty Images; p. 8 Kristopher Bell/Shutterstock.com; p. 9 Jeff Greenberg/Universal Images Group/Getty Images; p. 10 Putu Artana/Shutterstock.com; p. 11 John D Sirlin/Shutterstock.com; p. 12 Alta Oosthuizen/Shutterstock.com; p. 13 Courtesy of NASA; p. 15 Cary Meltzer/Shutterstock.com; p. 16 Christian Roberts-Olsen/Shutterstock.com; p. 17 Allan Davey/Moment/Getty Images; p. 19 IgorZh/Shutterstock.com; p. 21 (top) AFP Contributor/AFP/Getty Images; p. 21 (bottom) Vasin Lee/Shutterstock.com; p. 22 kornilov007/Shutterstock.com.

Cataloging-in-Publication Data

Names: Kingston, Seth.
Title: Lightning / Seth Kingston.
Description: New York : PowerKids Press, 2021. | Series: Lighting up the sky | Includes glossary and index.
Identifiers: ISBN 9781725318458 (pbk.) | ISBN 9781725318472 (library bound) | ISBN 9781725318465 (6 pack)
Subjects: LCSH: Lightning--Juvenile literature.
Classification: LCC QC966.5 K56 2021 | DDC 551.56'32--dc23

Manufactured in the United States of America

CPSIA Compliance Information: Batch #CSPK20. For Further Information contact Rosen Publishing, New York, New York at 1-800-237-9932.

CONTENTS

LOOK UP!

If you look up during a rainstorm, you might see a bright lightning bolt. A bolt of lightning often looks like a crack in the sky or an uneven staircase. Lightning is a **meteorological** event that occurs during thunderstorms. However, lightning can also strike during snowstorms and dust storms.

Lightning occurs when clouds give off extra electricity. Even though lightning is a beautiful part of nature, it's also dangerous and can cause fires, loss of power in homes, and even death. Later in this book you will learn how to stay safe if you see lightning.

If lightning strikes some types of sand, it may turn the sand into glass. The lightning is so hot that it melts the sand. These glass shapes are called fulgurites.

FULGURITE

THUNDER AND LIGHTNING

Thunder and lightning are closely linked. Every storm that has thunder also has lightning. In fact, lightning causes thunder to happen! When lightning occurs, it heats the air and causes it to **expand** quickly. This produces the sound we call thunder.

Thunderstorms form when wet, hot air rises and meets dry, cold air. As the warm air rises, it cools and forms water **vapor**, which **condenses** and makes a cloud. The higher the cloud goes, the colder the air becomes, forming ice. If the drops become heavy enough, they'll fall from the clouds down to the earth as **precipitation**.

SEEING THE LIGHT

The different thunder sounds we hear, such as rumbling, are caused by differences in the **atmosphere** and surface of the earth.

Some types of lightning
stay inside the clouds.

CHARGED UP!

Inside clouds, there are areas of positive and negative charges. The charges are on drops of water or ice crystals. Lighter drops of water and ice crystals gain a positive charge. Heavier ones gain a negative charge. When there's more of one type of charge, lightning forms.

Each year, the United States has more than 20 million lightning strikes that hit the ground. Most of these happen in Florida.

Negative charges gather in the middle of the cloud. Positive charges gather above and below the negatively charged area. Lightning is the electricity released when it becomes impossible for air to keep the charged areas apart. As a result, lightning occurs between oppositely charged areas, between charged areas and the ground, or between a charged area and the atmosphere.

CLOUD-TO-GROUND LIGHTNING

About one-third of lightning occurrences happen between the cloud and the ground. This type of lightning is called cloud-to-ground lightning. Cloud-to-ground lightning doesn't always hit the ground. It may strike homes, power lines, or even boats.

SEEING THE LIGHT

Lightning is unpredictable, meaning it's hard to guess where lightning will strike. Even though it's more likely for lightning to strike a tall object, lightning can strike anything.

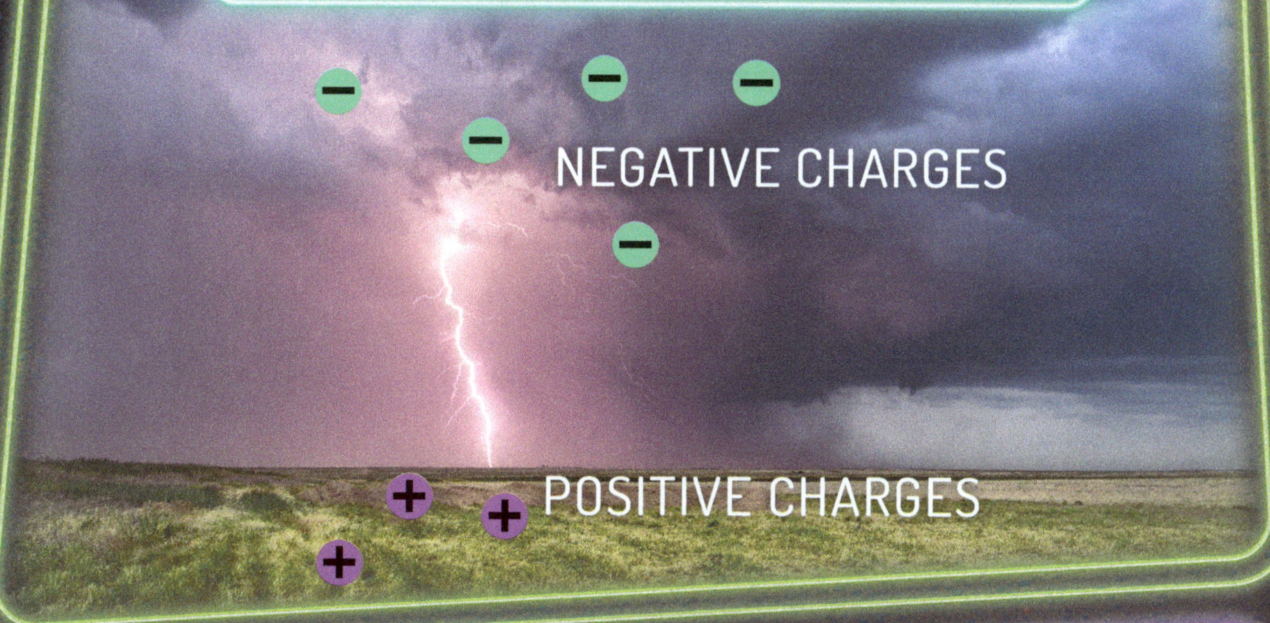

The negative charges in this cloud are attracted to the positive charges on the ground. The positive charges jump up to meet the negative charges. When they meet, the lightning goes back toward the cloud.

Cloud-to-ground lightning occurs when negative electrical charges inside a cloud build up while positive electrical charges on the ground beneath the cloud build up. These electrical charges are attracted to each other. As the cloud grows larger, the electrical charges carried on water droplets and ice crystals grow stronger. The cloud releases extra negative electrical charges. Lightning occurs when the opposite charges meet.

WHERE DOES LIGHTNING OCCUR?

Lightning occurs all over the world. Most lightning occurs over land, and only a small amount of lightning happens over the oceans. Most lightning happens in places near the **equator** because these areas experience more thunderstorms. In the Northern **Hemisphere**, many thunderstorms occur between May and September. Thunderstorms in the Southern Hemisphere are most common between November and March.

SEEING THE LIGHT

It's untrue that lightning doesn't strike in the same place twice. Today, scientists have found that lightning "needles" hit the same spot again and again. Lightning can even strike the same place again in a completely different storm.

Crewmembers aboard the International Space Station can sometimes see lightning from space! In this photograph, a line of storms moves through Asia on July 24, 2013.

Lake Maracaibo in northwestern Venezuela and the far eastern part of the Democratic Republic of the Congo in central Africa experience the most lightning anywhere in the world. This is because of where they are on Earth—close to the equator.

DIFFERENT KINDS OF LIGHTNING

Depending on where you are, you'll likely see different kinds of lightning. Lightning that occurs inside clouds often lights up the sky with a sheet of light. This is called sheet lightning. Heat lightning is lightning from a thunderstorm that's so far away you can't hear thunder.

A red sprite is red lightning that happens above storm clouds and can be miles long. A blue jet is cone-shaped lightning that glows blue. It happens above a storm's center and then travels up very quickly. Anvil lightning comes from the top part of the thunderstorm cloud, called the anvil, and travels straight down to the ground.

Keraunophobia is the fear of lightning or thunder.

AS FAST AS LIGHTNING!

In the blink of an eye, a lightning bolt can come and go. In fact, lightning can travel about 62,000 miles (99,760 km) per second. It's so fast we often can't tell when many lightning strikes have hit the same spot. To us, it just looks like one flickering lightning stroke.

SEEING THE LIGHT

Many species, or kinds, of plants and animals die when lightning causes bushfires and wildfires. Wildfires also cause people to have to evacuate, or leave, their homes.

In the United States, lightning causes an average of 9,000 wildfires each year.

Because lightning moves so fast, the damage it causes also happens quickly. Each lightning bolt can contain as many as 1 billion **volts** of electricity! It can heat the air around itself to five times hotter than the surface of the sun. Lightning often causes fires and may even split trees.

STRUCK BY LIGHTNING

People can die from being struck by lightning because the lightning causes their heart to stop beating. In the United States from 2009 to 2018, an average of 27 people a year died from lighting strikes. During that time, lightning injured an average of 243 people a year. If you see someone get struck by lightning, it's important you get them medical help as soon as possible.

People who survive being struck by lightning often have lasting health problems. In addition to burns, they may have memory loss, problems with their lungs and other body parts, or trouble sleeping.

SEEING THE LIGHT

About 90 percent of people struck by lightning survive. Depending on how badly they are injured, it may take them a long time to recover. However, they may never fully recover.

People who have been struck by lightning may join an online community of other lightning survivors. Survivors may also gather together to share their stories.

STAYING SAFE

A thunderstorm can happen quickly. As soon as you see storm clouds rolling in, feel rain, see lightning, or hear thunder, you should go somewhere safe. If you're outside, you should stay away from open areas such as sports fields and hiking trails.

Houses, malls, and other strong buildings are the safest places to be. Once inside, stay away from computers and TVs, as well as sinks and showers. They're all pathways through which electricity could travel.

If there's no shelter, you can put your feet close together and crouch, keeping your body close to the ground without touching it more than you must.

Even though it might seem OK to take shelter under a **pavilion** like these people are doing, you should do your best to find a house or other enclosed building.

BEFORE LIGHTNING STRIKES

Lightning seems to come from nowhere, but it may give you some warning signs before it strikes.

DARKENING SKIES	HIGH WINDS
RAINFALL	THUNDER
YOUR HAIR MAY STAND ON END	YOUR MOUTH MAY TASTE LIKE METAL

expand: To become bigger.

hemisphere: One-half of Earth.

meteorological: Having to do with meteorology, a science that deals with the atmosphere, weather, and weather forecasting.

pavilion: A building with open sides that is used as a place for entertainment or shelter in a park or garden.

precipitation: Water that falls to the ground as hail, mist, rain, sleet, or snow.

vapor: A substance in the form of a gas.

volt: A unit for measuring the force that moves an electric current.

INDEX

WEBSITES

Due to the changing nature of Internet links, PowerKids Press has developed an online list of websites related to the subject of this book. This site is updated regularly. Please use this link to access the list:
www.powerkidslinks.com/lus/lightning